IDENTITY

How To Live Life With Purpose and Fulfillment

Mary Cornelius Oudenga
Award-Winning Author

10-10-10
Publishing

Publisher
10-10-10 Publishing
Markham, ON Canada

Printed in Canada and the United States of America

Contents

Acknowledgments

I am grateful and thankful to God, the creator of the whole universe. He created us in his own image and likeness, to become like him and to continue the process of creation in us and through us. I thank God for sending his Son to come and die for us, and show us the way, the life, and the truth.

I am grateful to God's divine Holy Spirit who lives inside us and guides us to our divine helpers, so that we can fulfill his purpose in us and through us to advance his kingdom business on Earth.

Thanks to Raymond Aaron, Naval Kumar, Christiana Fife, Carrie Cunningham , Liz Ventrella, Lisa Browning, and the entire team for sharing your life experiences to help others achieve their goals of becoming authors, and authority in their calling to impact others in return, and continue the process for generations.

Thanks to prophet Lawrence Ausha, for setting the stage for my spiritual journey to my purpose. May God continue to use you in his kingdom business.

Thanks Bishop Samuel Pobi, the shepherd of my soul. Thank you for accepting me for who I am and believing in me even when I did not believe in myself. Thanks for leading by example and showing us that the future can be brighter than our past. Resurrected Life Church, a place where many become one! Words cannot express it all but God knows all.

Thanks to Kenneth Oudenga, my husband, for giving me opportunity, and freedom of becoming who God created me to be, and loving me the way I am in my strengths and weaknesses.

Thanks for your humility and always standing by my side.

Thank you for your love and teamwork in taking care of our parents until their last breath on Earth to a befitting burial. May God give you long life and prosperity in every area of your life holistically. Thanks for being a great husband, father, partner, and friend. May God who knows all things give you your heart's desires beyond what you can imagine.

I thank all my children, Bob Francis Okumu, Emmanuel Okumu, Victoria Oudenga, Gloria Oudenga, Elizabeth Faith Oudenga, and Rejoice Oudenga for making me a mother.

Thank you to all my godchildren, cousins, and spiritual sons and daughters. I am proud of you all in many ways. May God who knows all things give you your heart's desires according to his riches in glory through our Lord Jesus Christ.

My nephews and nieces, Sasuk Bonyo, Diania Bonyo, Kakiye Bonyo, Martin Bonyo, Grace Foutch, Marcus Ateib, Patience, Michelle, Jeremiah, Lia, Isaiah, Ella, Davion and so many more that I cannot name you all, but you are all in my heart.

To all my friends, family, parents at Mercy International Academy, Leadership at God's prayer line, Namusaala family, Kutas forum, Kumuri forum, Musalaba choir, Dirji Ru forum, Kingdom Life Empowerment forum, Good Samaritan forum, WALC, Word of Hope leadership, staff and volunteers at Holistic Medical Center, and Mercy Abundant Life Center, and communities in Nashville TN, and around the world plus more. Your encouragement, support, and prayers are highly appreciated.

Thank you to my parents. Thank you, Dad, for being my role model and mentor in kingdom business. Thanks for showing us to love God and others, and to live with integrity at all times, no matter who is watching. Thanks for helping us to work hard and to give to others as well. Thanks for your last words to live as the last day on Earth and to know who we are and to fight a good fight of faith in all life situations. You are both great leaders, role models, and mentors! RIP Dad.

Mom, thanks for your excellence and purity in spirit, as you stated you don't want anything to hinder your flow and relationship with God and the Holy Spirit. Thanks for teaching us to forgive in advance, regardless of the situation or no matter who is right. Thanks for showing me in action what real life and marriage is and to do our part with joy without complaining. Thanks for showing me how to make the Holy Spirit my best friend. I thought it was not necessary; I didn't catch some of your words but I now remember watching your life and your relationship with God, Dad, and us, and everyone is amazing.

I have witnessed your life; we talked about many things in the kingdom. This book is part of living that life you always talked about. Purpose and fulfillment until your last breath. Thanks for your last words, not your will but God's will to be done, and whatever that is good for God, let it be done in your life.

Mom and Dad, after your departure, your spirit was still talking loudly in Philippians 4:1-13 with verse 9 as my memory verse. It was very clear and loud to my spirit that we should not worry about you. You are at peace and enjoying yourselves in eternity but I should put what I have learned, seen, heard, and talked about and do it to many people! I will do my best with God's grace. You are both real heroes forever. RIP Mom, until we meet again in eternity.

Thanks to the Head Pastors Samuel, and Deborah Pobi, and resurrected church family leadership, partners, men, and women, youth, and children's ministries for all the great love, the spiritual, and prayer support during this journey.

- Apostle Precious, pastor Tanisha, and the Precious Crowns ministry internationally, Hendersonville TN
- Pastor Victor and Faith Nwakwo, Cleveland TN
- Pastor Martin Sudanese Community Church, Nashville TN
- Pastor William and Lady Nancy Boadi and the IGM Church family at large, Nashville TN
- Winner's lead pastors Francis and Lady Yankey and Winner's chapel family at large, Nashville TN
- Lead pastors of Holyhills Chapel, Prophet Nicky and First Lady, and the entire leadership and church at large in Murfreesboro TN
- Lead pastor and first lady Mills, Amazing Grace International in Knoxville TN
- Lead pastor and first lady, God's Agenda Church in Nashville TN
- Pastor and first lady, Spirit-Filled Church in Lavergne TN
- Lead pastor Chris and first lady Gina, Power House in Nashville TN
- Lead pastor Nkuruma and first lady Rosemary, Royal City Church International in Nashville TN
- All the church leaders, members, partners, and ministries around the world
- The government officials, families, and all businesses owners around the globe

About the Author

Mary Cornelius Oudenga is a Kingdom citizen, focused on the ways of God, who entered the earth through South Sudan Kuku by tribe but, due to the war in her country, was raised up in Uganda as a refugee. She relocated to the USA in 2005 with her parents and siblings, to join their step-sister Diko Cornelius who invited the family to join her in Nashville Tennessee.

Mary has lived in Nashville with her family since 2005, and met her husband Kenneth Oudenga in 2008. Both are committed members/ leaders of Resurrected Life Church Tennessee under the care and leadership of Bishop Samuel, and Pastor Deborah Pobi.

Mary is a proud wife, mom, daughter, friend, and caregiver/ nurse.

As a family child care provider, Mary has helped over thirteen nations to raise future leaders since 2016, currently with a medical clinic, Holistic Medical Center Kayunga, and an orphanage, Mercy Abundant Life Center, Kayunga District in Uganda.

With a goal of building a comprehensive school from nursery to high school plus more. Mary is also a proud daughter who started helping her mom with caring for her grandmother, children, and women on both sides, which was like indirect training and mentorship in her life.

She is blessed with her family,. her community, her spiritual parents as well Bishop Samuel Pobi Resurrected church family, and all those around her, She feels very grateful to have had her parents, and all the wealth of knowledge they passed on. After watching what happened to her biological parents, Mary realized that regardless of what we teach others, telling or documenting our stories is the best way to inspire others, and leave a lasting legacy for generations. For those who want to become authors.

You can reach her at loveintegrityfulfillment@gmail.com.

Foreword

Have you been searching for a way to strengthen your connection with God? Would you like to create a better version of yourself, and find a way to make that happen? Look no further, because *Identity – How to Live Life With Purpose and Fulfillment* is perfect for you. This book will help you understand your bond with God, and show you how to continuously improve it.

Mary Cornelius Oudenga has shared her own connection to the Lord, and has given you a chance to see all the good that God has provided for you. Each chapter has Bible verses that you can relate to, which can help you on your journey through life. You will find answers to some of the most frequently asked spiritual questions, as well as secrets to a successful and happy life. Mary gives you a way to ignite the fire within you, and bring yourself to the next level with God and the universe around you.

Everything happens for a reason, and you have reached this point on your journey because you were meant to. This is a great chance for you to reassess yourself and live life on purpose, without any regrets. Come join in this life of empowering others to find and achieve the same results of living life to the fullest, and doing all you can to not only better yourself for God, but help better others lives as well. When you live with unconditional Love for God, the possibilities are endless.

It is time for you to find not only your purpose, but your destiny. I highly recommend *Identity – How to Live Life With Purpose and Fulfillment* as a guide to creating a perfect balance in your life.

Raymond Aaron
***New York Times* Bestselling Author**

Introduction

I pray that, whatever your intentions in reading this book, God who knows all things will empower you to action and faith to achieve whatever you are destined for, and to live life with purpose and fulfillment in Jesus's name.

I wrote this book to share my testimony, life experiences, and lessons, and inspire you to enrich, enhance, encourage, empower, transform and leave your own legacy. Although my parents shared great wisdom when they were alive, I thought it was not important now since it's not written down or recorded, except to those who got close to them in many ways. But after their departure from this life, it's very hard to remember all of the great wisdom and knowledge that they shared with me, and were more than willing to share with everyone around them.

I tried to ask different people whom I thought were close to them, but it is not the same as hearing from them directly, and hard to get their wisdom. I have learned that we are the only people who are able to tell or document our stories, and to whomever we wish. It is important to do that, because we don't know how much time we have.

We are all gifted with many blessings.

Let's use our blessings to bless others so we can advance our Father's kingdom business on Earth. We still have the opportunity to make this world a better place before our transition to our permanent home in eternity. I want to encourage everyone that no matter what happens in our lives, there is still a way out if we don't give up.

Although our body looks complete, it's made up of many different parts. Just as a puzzle looks like one whole, it is made up of many different pieces. Let's not waste our pain. Let our pieces lead us to God's peace, purpose and gratitude for the lessons learned during the journey. When we trust God regardless of our situation, God can turn things around for our own good. (Romans 8:28)

The truth is that we like shortcuts, but these cut off some of the main pieces which are supposed to mold us to become our true self.

When I was in Africa, I wanted to go to school, but there was no money for school fees. I didn't know what to do. The only thing that came to mind was to end my life. I thought if I was not going to be able to go to school then my life had no benefits or use, two times, so it was better to end it. During my first attempt, I was not yet a Christian but went to church. I took an action but was saved by God's mercy and love.

During my second attempt, I was still in Africa, and already a Christian but I didn't know my purpose or who I was, before I took it further. I was listening to the radio and someone came through the air saying that it doesn't matter what you are going through, whether you are educated or not. She said that God has a plan for each and every one of us, regardless of where we are in life, educated or not educated. She defined "problems" as follows:

- Predict what's ahead of us
- Remind us that we can't do without God
- Opportunities that open new doors
- Blessings
- Lessons that we can learn from, when we have the right mindset

- Exist wherever we go; we cannot run away from problems
- Messages that we can use to encourage others
- Every problem we go through has solutions when we don't give up

During my third attempt, I was already in the USA, and was subject to a loved one's negative comments and judgment. When I was about to take action, I heard it clearly in my spirit, what does John 10:10 say? I did not need to read it because it was my favorite memory verse. The Bible stated that the Holy Spirit will teach us all truth and bring to our memories the word of God at the right time to deliver us from destruction and, as stated in John 10:10, the devil comes to steal, kill, and destroy but Jesus came to give us life and life abundantly till it overflows in all areas of our life when we trust him regardless of our situation as his word says to give thanks in all situations. When we know who we are in Christ it creates abundant life, purpose, and fulfillment.

We all have our personal definitions of identity, and it cannot be defined by the knowledge of where we came from, or background, how we portray ourselves or how others portray us; it's deeper than locations, and human understanding..

The following are questions to ponder:

- Where did we come from? What is our origin/foundation?
- Who are we? What is our identity?
- Why are we here? What is our purpose?
- What can we do while still here? What is our potential?
- Where are we going after here? What is our destiny?
- What can we be remembered for after our last breath? What is our legacy?

Chapter One

God the Father

"What God intended for you
goes far beyond anything you can imagine."
— Oprah Winfrey

1

The Origin

**"And God saw everything that he had made,
and, behold, it was very good."
(Genesis 1:31)**

G od's original plan was created out of love. He as the Father wanted a place for his children. He wanted a home … a place of safety for all who he loved, and for all who loved him. This is all explained throughout Genesis chapter one to the end of chapter two. From the beginning, God created heaven and the earth with his word and out of love. God prepared or created everything that we needed so we could live a life of purpose and fulfillment.

He made a world that is capable of carrying billions and billions of people, and for those people, he created water and food so that each generation could not only survive, but also flourish. Though this was not the first "beginning" as God makes it clear that other worlds have passed away, when it says in Genesis (1:1), "In the beginning…", this was the beginning of this world … our world, and he made it for us, and so we would be happy and healthy.

God is so great he was able to create this world in just seven days. On day one, God created light when before there was only darkness. He said, "Let there be light." (Genesis 1:3)

On day two, he created the heavens and earth. He divided the atmosphere in two so it was perfectly equal (Genesis 1:6). He wanted a world that was both beautiful and safe for all living beings.

On day three, God created plants that gave us the ability to survive. He created separation between land and water so humans had a place to build and grow. He wanted to secure our survival, so he ensured we had everything we could ever need. (Genesis 1:9)

On day four, he gave us the moon ... the stars ... and all the seasons. He wanted a place of beauty. He wanted us to see the skies above us ... to see the stars and moon sparkle in the night. He created a perfect home for us all. (Genesis 1:14)

On day five, he created the sea creatures in the water, and birds in the sky. He gave them the ability to reproduce so that their kind could grow, and helps humans to survive and flourish. (Genesis 1:23)

On day six, he created all animals and creatures to help us as humans survive and have food to eat. Not only did he create all animals on this day, he also created man. He made us perfect. He made us in his image. (Genesis 1:27)

God the Holy Spirit created man in his own image and likeness. He let them have complete authority over every living thing that creeps upon the earth. So, God created man in his image, and in the image and likeness of God he created them male and female.

Genesis 1:26-27: Then God said, "Let Us (Father, Son, Holy Spirit) make man in Our image, according to Our likeness (not physical, but a spiritual personality and moral likeness); let them have complete authority over the fish of the sea, the birds of the air, the cattle, over the entire earth, and over everything that creeps *and* crawls on the earth."

1:27 - So God created man in His own image, in the image *and* likeness of God He created him; male and female He created them."

Psalms 104:30 - "You send out your Spirit, they are created; you renew the face of the ground."

Day seven was the final day, and it was meant for rest. It was and still is the Holy Day. In this time, he continued to perfect man and the vegetation in the world. He wanted to ensure this world would be one that would last.

The Word

In the beginning (before all time), was the word (Christ). The word was with God, and the word was God himself, which means we cannot separate from His word. In order for us to know God and ourselves, we need to know His word as well.

He was present with God ... **John 1:1-5, 1:1 - "In the beginning (before all time) was the word (Christ), and the word was with God, and the word was God Himself."**

1:2 - He was [continually existing] in the beginning [co-eternally] with God.

1:3 - All things were made *and* came into existence through Him; and without Him not even one thing was made that has come into being.

1:4 - In Him was life [and the power to bestow life], and the life was the Light of men.

1:5 - The Light shines on in the darkness, and the darkness did not understand it *or* overpower it *or* appropriate it *or* absorb it [and is unreceptive to it]."

Although it is clear we should follow God's word, it is sometimes unclear what exactly his word is. In Timothy 3:16-3:17, it says that, "All Scripture is God-breathed and is useful for teaching, rebuking, correcting and training in righteousness, so that the servant of God may be thoroughly equipped for every good work."

God's word is meant to teach us and help lead us to the path of righteousness. It is meant to teach us the right way to take in life, and how to be caring, helpful, and good people. The Bible is ageless. It is something that can be looked back on and used, no matter what year passes us. God's word is never meant to fade or go away. It is meant to stay permanently engrained in our minds as a way to guide us.

(Psalm 119:105) "Your word is a lamp for my feet, a light on my path."

His word is meant to give us answers that will better our lives. Even though he is not visibly next to us, his word is meant to be the warmth you need when you are looking for the right path to take. His word is there to help remind you he is always next to you ... always here trying to show us our worth, and our purpose.

(Isaiah 40:8) "The grass withers and the flowers fall, but the word of our God ensures forever."

No matter how much time has passed, and how distant you may feel from God, just know his word never fades. It stays as the seasons pass, and as you age each year. His word is meant to never leave your mind, because no matter where you are, or how far you have fallen, God is there waiting to pick you up again.

Now, since we have some foundation of our origin and God's word, let's start by defining who God is.

God the Father

God is the Father to us all. No matter who you are, you are a child of God, and he made you perfectly in his image. He cares for us all, and ensures every creature of his is cared for. He wants all of us to follow the right path, and to serve him, and despite some of us losing our way, he still is there waiting for us to come back to him. He loves us no matter what we do, and that is the purest love of all. He is there for us every step of the way, and even though you cannot see him, he is there for you.

(Isaiah 64:7) – "Yet, Lord, you are our father; we are the clay and you our potter: we are all the work of your hand."

We are the image of God's word. We are the result of God's work and the effort he has made. We are molded by what he wants for us, and we as his children are the ones who should continue to share his word, and do the work he requires of us. He gave us the beautiful land we stand on, and the creatures that ensure our survival, so we need to do everything we can as his children to keep spreading his word, and keep helping him create a better tomorrow, and the process continues.

(Luke 6:35-36) – "But love your enemies, do good, and lend, expecting nothing in return. Your reward will be great, and you will be children of the Most High; for he is kind to the ungrateful and the wicked. Be merciful, just as your Father is merciful."

God has always given us mercy and forgiveness. He wants us to be happy, and make the right decisions, but even when we falter, he is still there waiting for us to find our way again. He loves us all and does not discriminate. He is the guide that we should follow. He is the great one who cares for each and every living thing no matter what they may have done. He equally cares for us all as we should care for him and the words he has shared with us.

We should strive to live like God, and be someone he would be proud of.

God our Father is the reason we are here, and the reason we should be thankful for the lives we have. He is everything: *the I am that I am* . He is love, peace, and all we can think of. He is the ground we walk on. He created all we see, which is why we should always follow God's word and understand who he is and why he gave us this amazing life we all live.

Love

(1 John 4:8) "The one who does not love has not become acquainted with God [does not and never did know Him], for God is love. [He is the originator of love, and it is an enduring attribute of His nature.]"

God is the creator of all; therefore, he is the creator of love. Without God, we would not have the ability to express such emotions as love, and with him being the person that gave us life, he is the first to have shown us love. He is the one who cares for us all no matter what we do. No matter what mistake we make, we are still his children, and he loves us unconditionally. If you want to truly understand love, you need to first look at all God has done for you, and how he has expressed his love for all his children.

(1 John 3:1) "See what great love the Father has lavished on us, that we should be called children of God! And that is what we are! The reason the world does not know us is that it did not know him."

God loved us so much that he gave us a world filled with vegetation so we had oxygen to breathe, and plants to harvest and eat. He gave us water so we would not be thirsty. He gave us animals so we could eat and also learn to care for smaller beings. He gave us beautiful landscapes to look at. And not only did he give us all the parts of our world, he also gave us amazing minds that allow us to think and learn new things. He loved us that much that he gave us all these wonderful objects and abilities.

Through his teachings of love, his plan for us is to keep sharing that love with others. He created love so it could grow and be passed on to others. Love is not something that should end … it is something that should continuously flourish.

(1 John 4:7) "Dear friends, let us love one another, for love comes from God. Everyone who loves has been born of God and knows God."

The world is not meant to be filled with hate. We are all meant to love one another, and learn to truly understand each other's differences and come to accept them. God made us all unique and special in our own way, and he did not do this to have other people focus on those differences and judge. He made us different so we can see the beauty in every individual. We are not supposed to look down upon one another; instead, we should be uplifting people and living the way God would want us to. We should be loving each other just as God loves us.

Why stay in the darkness when you can walk into the light and see the purest love that you could ever feel? Once you truly feel that love for God, you will want to share it because you will know how life-changing it can be. If we were all just a little kinder to one another, the world would start to be a better place. If the kindness grew, then God's love could also continue to grow, and ultimately, I think that is all he wants for us. He wants us to be like him and represent him to those who still don't know him. (2 Corinthians 5;17-20)

Notes

_____

_____

_____

_____

_____

_____

_____

_____

_____

_____

_____

_____

_____

Chapter Two

God the Son

"True leaders don't invest in buildings. Jesus never built a building. They invest in people. Why? Because success without a successor is failure. So, your legacy should not be in buildings, programs, or projects; your legacy must be in people."
— Myles Munroe

Our Savior

"I and the Father are one."
(John 10:30)

J esus, the son of God, and also known as our Savior, was born to help teach us the word of God, and to let us all know the importance of it, and why we should listen. Jesus was meant to help people on Earth understand who the Lord is and why he is such a crucial part of our lives. He is one with God and God is one with him.

Our Savior was brought down to our world to help guide us and teach us the right way to live. He showed us what it meant to worship the Lord, and live our lives in the way he always imagined. While God cannot be with us in a visual sense, Jesus is a way to connect with him and help you to see that he is there always helping us along our path; always leading the way.

(John 6:29) *Jesus answered, "The work of God is this: to believe in the one he has sent."*

God had the Savior come down to us so we could believe in him. Since Jesus and God are one, the Lord wants us to believe in Jesus as much as we believe in the Lord. If God's word is true, then Jesus' word is also true. We are meant to follow the path of God

... the path of righteousness so we can end our life knowing that we will be brought up to the heavens to finally meet God and the one who saved us all. Our life on Earth is only the beginning, and when we truly stay connected with God and our Savior, we are guaranteed to have a beautiful here and in the afterlife ... one where God is by our side.

(John 14:6) *"I am the way and the truth and the life. No one comes to the Father except through me"*

In John 14:6, Jesus states that no one else can reach out to the Father and communicate with him other than himself. He is the only connection to God, which is why the word of our Savior is also the word of our Lord. They are connected as one. They know the right path we should take as we are all God's children just as Jesus is.

Jesus was born into our world to help spread the word, and help teach us the right way to live. Even if we do not listen to his guidance, he is always there waiting for us to find our way again. You see, our Savior never leaves our side despite the bad things we may do. He is always there to guide us back to the path we were meant to be on. That is the divine love of both our Lord and Savior.

(John 14:1) *"Do not let your hearts be troubled. Trust in God; trust also in me."*

Have you ever felt unsure about yourself or the journey you are on? This may be a sign that the Savior is trying to help you find your way again. When you trust in God, as well as the word of his son, you will no longer have that feeling of being unsure or troubled. Instead, your path will become clear and you will no longer question what the Lord wants for you. When you trust in the plan that was made for you, that is when you fully feel God's love, and the love of his son. That is when you no longer question where you are and where your life is meant to take you.

(John 3:18) *"Whoever believes in him is not condemned, but whoever does not believe stands condemned already because they have not believed in the name of God's one and only Son."*

Believing in God and the words of his son ensures that you have them by your side every step of the way. They want nothing more than to help you find your way, and give you a life that is full of health and happiness. Despite the pain they may feel from you losing your way, the Lord and the Savior are there waiting for you to come back to them. They never give up on you, and that is the truest form of love. They love you no matter how far you may have fallen.

The Savior's purpose is to let you know that, no matter what, God is there for you, and God will stay there for you. He will be there on your darkest days. He will be there for you when you feel like you may not need him. God is always there, and his son is always there to remind you.

Love

(1 Corinthians 13:4-7) *"Love is patient and kind; love does not envy or boast; it is not arrogant or rude. It does not insist on its own way; it is not irritable or resentful; it does not rejoice at wrongdoing, but rejoices with the truth. Love bears all things, believes all things, hopes all things, endures all things."*

The love from God and his son is the strongest and purest of all. Their love is patient and never-ending. They do not judge, nor do they have negative opinions of you. That is because you are a part of them, as all God's children are. His love is meant to conquer all, and guide you through your life. His love is there to show you that you are never alone and that, no matter what, you will have someone watching over you.

This is what love should be. It should be unconditional and should never be something that will fade. Love is a way to show others that they are important and they are cared about. We should all try to express our love the way God, and the son of God, do because their love is one that you will feel with every step you take. Their love is one that will stay with you even when you have lost your way.

(John 15:1) *"I am the true vine, and my Father is the gardener."*

In John 15:1, Jesus, the son of God, states that he is the vine, and God the Father is the gardener. When he said this, he meant that God is the gardener taking care of us all, and ensuring that the vine and branches are well cared for. The vine carries all its knowledge to the branches, ensuring that they are successful and happy in life. Without a healthy strong vine, we being the branches would just wither away and would follow a path of wrongdoing.

Jesus, our vine, is there to show us the way and give us the love we need. He is there to let us know who our Father is, and why we are meant to follow him. You see, there is no greater love than the one we get from God above, and Jesus is here to help give us that love and let us know that his love will never fade.

(John 15:9) *"As the Father has loved me, so have I loved you. Now remain in my love."*

(John 15:12) *"My command is this: Love each other as I have loved you."*

Both God and the son of God do not want the love to stop when it comes to you. They want the love to continue to spread throughout all people so that every single person can understand God's love and feel it first-hand. When we learn true love, we only want to spread it to others we care about. So, follow in the word of God and strive to love each and every person you see. Do not give hate, and understand that no matter how lost someone may be, there is always a way to bring them back, and love is the first step.

The Word

(John 1:14) *"The Word became flesh and made his dwelling among us. We have seen his glory, the glory of the one and only Son, who came from the Father, full of grace and truth."*

While you cannot physically hear the son of God speaking God's word and his own, you can hear them throughout the Bible. Their wants and needs for us are written on each page, and in each word. Just like God, Jesus only wants us to be happy and follow a path that will lead us to the Father.

Not only can you hear the words of the Lord and his son, you can know that they are listening. Each prayer you say, and every thought you have ... they are in you, and by your side helping you to heal or come to a solution. I know at times you may question if Jesus and the Father are still guiding you, especially if you are going through hardship, but just know that there is a plan for you, and while that plan may cause some challenges, that is what is meant for you and the journey you are on. God gave you life, and gave you what you could handle. He knew you would come out a stronger person, just like his son.

(John 17:17) *"Sanctify them by the truth; your word is the truth."*

(John 5:19) *Jesus gave them this answer: "Very truly I tell you, the Son can do nothing by himself; he can do only what he sees his Father doing, because whatever the Father does the Son also does."*

You can believe Jesus' words because they are the word of the Lord. They are the answers you have been searching for. And if you ever need them ... do not look far. They are in the air you breathe, the roots in the trees, the water that fills our oceans, and the souls that are within all of us. When you pray, they are listening, and Jesus is the connection that keeps us all together.

The Way

(John 6:35) *Then Jesus declared, "I am the bread of life. Whoever comes to me will never go hungry, and whoever believes in me will never be thirsty."*

You will always know that you are following the way of the Lord if you are following his son. As Jesus says, he is the bread of life. He sacrificed his own life so that we could have ours. He is the reason that you are standing here today, so there is no reason for you to doubt his word or the path he has made for you. Choose to love him like he has loved you for so long. Give him the joy of knowing that you are living your life in God's way, and choosing to follow the path of righteousness.

While you have an endless life in the spiritual world once you reach heaven, you only have one physical life. Instead of living it in shame, follow the path of the Lord just as his son did. Be happy, healthy, and honest.

(John 3:17) *"For God did not send his Son into the world to condemn the world, but to save the world through him."*

(John 8:12) *When Jesus spoke again to the people, he said, "I am the light of the world. Whoever follows me will never walk in darkness, but will have the light of life."*

Notes

_____

_____

_____

_____

_____

_____

_____

_____

_____

_____

_____

_____

_____

_____

_____

Notes

Chapter Three
God the Holy Spirit

"In truth, I have done nothing alone.
God has called me and has been my pilot. The Holy Spirit has
been my comforter, my guide, and my power source."
— Reinhard Bonnke

3

The 3rd Personality of God

**"God is spirit, and those who worship Him
must worship in spirit and truth."
(John 4:24)**

Throughout the Bible, and through us understanding who the Lord is, we have come to see that he shows himself in different ways. He shows himself in the physical form, in spiritual form, as well as through just connecting with us and the souls within us all. He has no limitations because he is the Almighty. And when it comes to the different dimensions or personalities of being with the spirit, each give you a different perspective and a different reason to love him and worship him.

First Dimension: The first dimension, which is also known as his "omnipresence," is the spiritual being of God. It is the one that surrounds us no matter where we are and what we are doing. He is everywhere. This is why he can hear all our prayers, our thoughts, and our wants and needs. He is there even when we cannot feel him or see him. You are always in the hands of God as his spirit carries him everywhere.

(Revelation 1:10) "I was in the Spirit on the Lord's day, and heard behind me a great voice, as of a trumpet."

Second Dimension: The second dimension, or the "indwelling" presence, is referring to God being within all of us. Within the Bible, you will read about God being in the body of a mortal man. He can be within us to guide us, and help us find our way if we are lost. He does not discriminate, and he loves all. We are all the children of God, so we are all fully connected to him.

(1 Corinthians 3:16) *"Do you not know that you are the temple of God and that the Spirit of God dwells in you?"*

Third Dimension: This is also known as his "manifest" presence. As you know, throughout the Bible, God manifests himself in many different ways, including through water, wind, thunder, rainbows, or even an audible voice, a vision or dream. He can see all, and he can do all. He is all.

(Acts 2:2) *"And suddenly there came from heaven a sound like a mighty rushing wind, and it filled the entire house where they were sitting."*

While not all have seen God, most have felt his presence. They have felt warmth touch their hand, answers come into their mind, and a relief come over their body. God is there when you least expect him .... Even when you think you may not need him, he is there. He is the wind blowing through the trees, the sun beaming on your face, and the waves collecting on the water. You never have to worry about the path you are on because God has a plan for you, and he is there with you every step of the way.

(John 1:8) *"No one has ever seen God, but the one and only Son, who is himself God and is in closest relationship with the Father, has made him known."*

Fruits of the Spirit

(Isaiah 11:2) *"The Spirit of the LORD will rest on him— the Spirit of wisdom and of understanding, the Spirit of counsel and of might, the Spirit of the knowledge and fear of the LORD."*

God once said that we are known by our fruit, and what he meant by this is that we have the ability to be good and live a life of righteousness. Having the fruits of the spirit means you are turning away from evil, and choosing to walk with God, and follow in his ways.

Below are the nine fruits of the spirit:

1. **Love**
   Within **Galatians 5:22-23**, love comes from the Greek word "agape," and while the Greek language may have different ways of saying love, "agape" is considered perfect love, and only one that God can give you. It is the deep love you feel with God, and the connection that can never be broken. And when you love others in the way that God loves you, that is when you are closest to him.

2. **Joy**
   Joy in this passage is χαρά. Chara is often translated as joy or delight. It often is seen in the Bible with gladness. It is the realization of God's favor and grace in one's life. Biblical joy is happiness that is not dependent on our circumstances.

3. **Peace**
   The Biblical concept of peace, εἰρήνη (eirene) in Greek, is inclusive of life without conflict, as well as wholeness and harmony with God and others. A life of peace is safe and secure

both physically, mentally. and spiritually.

"The mind governed by the flesh is death, but the mind governed by the Spirit is life and peace." (Romans 8:6)

Peace results from allowing the Holy Spirit to work in our hearts and minds. When we have peace, we are from fear and worry about finances, our safety, our salvation, and our eternal life. The fruit of the Holy Spirit is seen in the peace that comes even when our circumstances are far from tranquil. Jesus encouraged his followers in John 16:33, *"I have told you these things, so that in me you may have peace. In this world you will have trouble. But take heart! I have overcome the world."*

4. Forbearance

Forbearance μακροθυμία (makrothumia) is not a word that most of us commonly use. The Greek word in Galatians 5:22-23 is often translated using other words such as patience, endurance, constancy, steadfastness, perseverance, long-suffering, and slowness in avenging wrongs. The Holy Spirit empowers believers to withstand challenging situations with perseverance and endurance.

The Greek root of this word relates to two words that mean long and passion. Through the Holy Spirit, we are able to wait longer before indulging our passions—we become "long-tempered" rather than "short-tempered." Paul used this word when he was describing Jesus' patience (μακροθυμία) with him.

5. **Kindness**

   Kindness χρηστότης (chréstotés) conveys the meaning of moral goodness, integrity, usefulness, and benignity. In the King James version of the Bible, this word is translated as "gentleness," which links it to the meaning of a gentleman or a gentlewoman who behaved properly, with moral integrity and kindness.

   Romans 2:4 reminds us that God's mercy and grace should lead us to repentance, not judgment. The Holy Spirit enables us to have moral integrity with kindness and not get trapped in self-righteous judgment.

6. **Goodness**

   Goodness ἀγαθωσύνη (agathosune) means uprightness of heart and life, goodness, and kindness. Goodness is seen in our actions. This word relates to not only being good but also doing good things.

   The Contemporary English version of 2 Thessalonians 1:11 highlights this meaning, *"We pray for God's power to help you do all the good things you hope to do and your faith makes you want to do."* Through the Holy Spirit's work in Christians' lives, they are upright in the heart and do good things.

7. **Faithfulness**

   Faithfulness πίστις (pistis) is evidence of the Holy Spirit's work in our lives. Faithfulness is a character trait that combines dependability and trust based on our confidence in God and his eternal faithfulness.

In the New Testament, faith is the belief in God, and the conviction that Jesus is the Messiah through whom we obtain eternal salvation.

8. Gentleness

Gentleness πρᾳΰτης (prautes) was translated as "meekness" in the King James version, but because being meek seemed weak, modern translations of the Bible use gentleness to mean mildness of disposition.

Baker's Evangelical Bible Dictionary explains, "Meekness does not identify the weak but more precisely the strong who have been placed in a position of weakness where they persevere without giving up. The use of the Greek word when applied to animals makes this clear, for it means 'tame' when applied to wild animals. In other words, such animals have not lost their strength but have learned to control the destructive instincts that prevent them from living in harmony with others."

9. Self-Control

Self-control ἐγκράτεια (egkrateia) is the ability to control one's body and its sensual appetites and desires – physically and mentally – through the power of the Holy Spirit. Self-control relates to both chastity and sobriety, particularly moderation in eating and drinking. Self-control is the opposite of the works of the flesh that indulge sensual desires.

(Matthew 12:22) "Either make the tree good and its fruit good, or make the tree bad and its fruit bad, for the tree is known by its fruit."

In the above verse (Matthew 12:22), it says that one should either make the tree good and its fruit good, or make the tree bad and its fruit bad, for the tree is known by its fruit. What is meant by this is that each person either has the choice to follow in the word of the Lord as well as the fruits of the spirit, or to go against it. You can either choose a path of good, and live your life to serve God, or you can choose to take the path of evil, and make poor decision after poor decision.

God does not make a choice for us ... He lets us decide all on our own. While he wants the best for all of us, and wants us to follow his path, we ultimately need to make that decision. When you learn to take care of your tree, and strive to make good fruit though, that spreads, and makes others want to follow suit.

(1 Timothy 1:17) *"Now to the King eternal immortal, invisible, the only God, be honor and glory for ever and ever. Amen."*

Teacher

(Psalm 143:10) *"Teach me to do your will, for you are my God; may your good Spirit lead me on level ground."*

We all have teachers throughout our life. In school, you had teachers who helped you understand the basics of life, and got you on our way to the next step. At home, you had parents who cared for you and taught you what was right and wrong. It does not matter who you are; along the way, you had people who assisted you and guided you so you knew the right path to take, as well as what would give you the best life. Well, are you ready to hear about the greatest teacher of all?

I know you have heard of him as we have been discussing him quite extensively so far. Our ultimate and most powerful teacher is our almighty Lord. He is the one who first taught us right and wrong. He was the one who made it clear the life he wanted for all of us, and he strived to give us a world that we would be successful in. He is the teacher that knows all. Our teachers on Earth only know what is inside them because of God. We are all just his children teaching others how what path to follow. Each generation is another generation of God's teachers, but he is the first and the best of all generations.

His purpose in sharing all the knowledge he has is to ensure that each of his children is happy and healthy, and follows a path that is right for them. He does not discriminate … He teaches all no matter what they may have done. Remember, there is nowhere God is not; he is there teaching you every single step of your life. His spirit helps you in every moment, and reminds you the importance of his teachings.

God is truly amazing!

(Psalm 139:7) *"Where can I go from your Spirit? Where can I flee from your presence?"*

Comforter

(Isaiah 31:3) *"But the Egyptians are mere mortals and not God; their horses are flesh and not spirit. When the Lord stretches out his hand, those who help will stumble, those who are helped will fall; all will perish together."*

As I have mentioned throughout the book so far, God can do all. He is our helper, our guider, our voice when we can't speak, our teacher, our comforter, and so much more.

He is there even when we you do not need him because he is always waiting to be that comfort for you. He is your helping hand in the dark, and your shade from the light. He is that feeling inside you when you have felt so lost and down for some time, and you finally have release.

He is there for you, and all he wants in return is for you to be there for him. He wants you to spread his word, and share the light that he gives you. He does not ask for money or any material object because all he wants is your love and acceptance.

(Acts 7:48-50) *However, the Most High does not live in houses made by human hands. As the prophet says: "Heaven is my throne, and the earth is my footstool. What kind of house will you build for me? says the Lord. Or where will my resting place be? Has not my hand made all these things?"*

Just look around you. God gave you the ground you stand on. He gave you the home you live in. The food you eat. He gave all this to you so that you could have a good life, and be happy. He wants only the best for all of us, and you can see that just by looking at the beautiful earth we live on. He did this all for us.

If he can do all of this for us, what we can do for him is continue to spread the comfort that he gives us. Be the helping hand someone else needs. If someone is hungry, give them food. If someone is thirsty, bring them water. Simple things can create a beautiful future.

Counselor

(Hebrews 4:12) *"For the word of God is alive and active. Sharper than any double-edged sword, it penetrates even to dividing soul and spirit, joints and marrow; it judges the thoughts and attitudes of the heart."*

I am sure within your life, you had received some form of counsel, or advice. Perhaps it was a parent who gave you advice on what school you should attend, or what career you should venture into. Maybe it was a friend who was worried about you. The first counselor in your life has always been God though. He was there before you were even brought into the physical world. And while you cannot physically see him or hear his voice, he is always listening to you, and giving you advice internally.

When it comes to looking for answers in your own life, he can be the inner voice you hear in your head. He can be the intuition you feel when something doesn't feel right. He is all around us, and is the one who gives us what we need.

You see, the Lord does not judge any of us. No matter what we have done in our lives, he is always there to guide us and help us through our problems. He loves us all unconditionally, and while human beings look at the outward appearance of others, God looks internally. He looks at the heart and soul, and sees us all as his children.

If you ever need counsel, know that you do not have to look far for He is already listening, and waiting to give you the answers you need. His spirit flows through all of us, and can be with us all at once. There are no limitations for God, and no limitations to what he can do. Never feel alone for he is there, and when you truly need someone to speak to, he is the truest counselor.

(1 Samuel 16:7) *But the Lord said to Samuel, "Do not consider his appearance or his height, for I have rejected him. The Lord does not look at the things people look at. People look at the outward appearance, but the Lord looks at the heart."*

Notes

_____

_____

_____

_____

_____

_____

_____

_____

_____

_____

_____

_____

_____

_____

_____

_____

Notes

_____

_____

_____

_____

_____

_____

_____

_____

_____

_____

_____

_____

_____

_____

Chapter Four

Identity

*"God's greatest attribute is not his power,
though it is omniscience; not his glory,
though it is burning majesty: it is his love."*
— Al Bryant

Who We Are In Christ

**"Therefore, if anyone is in Christ, he is a new creation.
The old has passed away; behold, the new has come."
(2 Corinthians 5:17-21) - 17**

18 All this is from God, who through Christ reconciled us to himself and gave us the ministry of reconciliation;

19 that is, in Christ God was reconciling the world to himself, not counting their trespasses against them, and entrusting to us the message of reconciliation.

20 Therefore, we are ambassadors for Christ, God making his appeal through us. We implore you on behalf of Christ, be reconciled to God.

21 For our sake he made him to be sin who knew no sin, so that in him we might become the righteousness of God.

Have you ever taken the time to wonder why you are the way you are? What makes you individually you? Well, it shouldn't surprise you that you are perfectly you because of God, our Father. He is the one who created you and gave you the life you wake up to each day. He is the one who has loved you since even before your existence, and he will keep loving you for all eternity.

Even if you have faltered, or made mistakes, God is still there for you. Can you believe that? God is so forgiving that he will stand by your side no matter what you have done in your past. He is there for you every step of the way, and all he asks of you is that you continue to spread his word. He wants every single person in this universe to know his name and to know what he has done for us all.

Just look around you … the beauty of the world is everywhere for you to see. He made it all just for us. He wanted to give us a world so amazing that we would all be safe and happy. His love is so great that he would do absolutely anything for us, and he shows us this on a daily basis.

Miracles happen every single day, and they are all thanks to our Almighty Lord. Not only has he given us a beautiful world to live in, he has given each and every one of us life, and a chance at creating the future we all have wanted. You are not alone in this. You are God's child just like everyone else, and while you may not see it at times, he wants you to live life to the fullest, and be happy every step of the way. He does not feel anger for your mistakes, and he forgives you like no other.

Stop waiting for life to start. You are already there, and you have the chance to spread the word of the Lord so you can better your life, and the lives of others around you. The word of the Lord is so pure and wonderful; it is truly life-changing if you accept his word and strive to spread it.

Keep believing in him, and in yourself. I know I believe in you, as well as the power that God holds. When you keep pushing to believe, that is when your path becomes clearest. That is when you know you are in God's hands.

(Romans 10:8) – "But what does it say? "The word is near you;

it is in your mouth and in your heart," that is, the word of faith we are proclaiming."

Moving Away From Materials or Objects

(2 Corinthians 5:7-21) - [7] For we live by faith, not by sight.

[8] We are confident, I say, and would prefer to be away from the body and at home with the Lord.

[9] So we make it our goal to please him, whether we are at home in the body or away from it.

[10] For we must all appear before the judgment seat of Christ, so that each of us may receive what is due us for the things done while in the body, whether good or bad.

The Ministry of Reconciliation

[11] Since, then, we know what it is to fear the Lord, we try to persuade others. What we are is plain to God, and I hope it is also plain to your conscience.

[12] We are not trying to commend ourselves to you again, but are giving you an opportunity to take pride in us, so that you can answer those who take pride in what is seen rather than in what is in the heart.

[13] If we are "out of our mind," as some say, it is for God; if we are in our right mind, it is for you.

[14] For Christ's love compels us, because we are convinced that one died for all, and therefore all died.

[15] And he died for all, that those who live should no longer live for themselves but for him who died for them and was raised again.

¹⁶ So from now on we regard no one from a worldly point of view. Though we once regarded Christ in this way, we do so no longer.

¹⁷ Therefore, if anyone is in Christ, the new creation has come: The old has gone, the new is here!

¹⁸ All this is from God, who reconciled us to himself through Christ and gave us the ministry of reconciliation:

¹⁹ that God was reconciling the world to himself in Christ, not counting people's sins against them. And he has committed to us the message of reconciliation.

²⁰ We are therefore Christ's ambassadors, as though God were making his appeal through us. We implore you on Christ's behalf: Be reconciled to God.

²¹ God made him who had no sin to be sin for us, so that in him we might become the righteousness of God.

In the modern society we live in, it seems to be far more common now to focus on the material side of things. We all look for the next new item, or the newest trend. We are always striving to look better, look younger, and make more money on top of it all. Sadly, we have become far too focused on materials instead of what truly matters, and that is just caring for others, and the world we live in.

God did not create this beautiful and magical universe to have us forget about his word. He gave us the land we walk on, the water we drink, and the food we eat so we can continue to spread his word generation after generation, and despite the millions of objects surrounding us, we are meant to stay focused and not falter. We are meant to live a good and righteous life; one that our Father would be proud of.

(Matthew 5:12) – "Rejoice and be glad, for your reward is great in heaven, for so men persecuted the prophets who were before you."

Why are you waiting for answers to come to you when the answers have already been given? He has made it clear what he wants us to do with our lives. There are no clouds covering his words. All you need to do is look within you, and talk with him. He will help you understand what is truly important.

(1 Peter 2:9) – "But you are a chosen people, a royal priesthood, a holy nation, God's special possession, that you may declare the praises of him who called you out of darkness into his wonderful light."

You are one of the lucky chosen ones. You are part of his family. You are intertwined into the endless generations of lucky souls who have been blessed with the Lord's presence and guidance. He has brought you out of the darkness so you could live a beautiful life in the light. One where you can help spread the news of the Lord, and His word. One where you can feel at peace in your mind, body, soul, and spirit.

Share his love with others as he has shown you. His love is not meant to stop with you ... it is meant to be spread throughout the entire world. His love is your love, and your love is your neighbor's love. It is an ever-flowing stream that continues to change the lives of others, and help them to understand their own journey and reason for living.

If you do not share the love of God with others, than you do not truly know who God is. You are nothing more than a stranger to him because he is the purest source of love. If you do not feel that warmth from his love and care, then maybe it's time you re-connect with him. Do not be shy. He remembers you, and has always been waiting for you to come back to him. Learn to know love because then, you will truly know God.

(1 John 4:8) – "Anyone who does not love does not know God, because God is love."

Acknowledging and Accepting Who You Are

(1 Peter 2:8-21) – "A stone that causes people to stumble and a rock that makes them fall. They stumble because they disobey the message - which is also what they were destined for."

Learning to acknowledge and accept who you are is not always automatic. We all have moments where we question who we are, and where we are going in life. That is perfectly natural. We all have doubts in our mind that at times take over and make it difficult to get back on the right path. Do not be afraid though, dear friend, for you are connected to the most powerful being in the entire universe. You are one of God's children and you are cared for just like all his children are.

While you may not see yourself in the best light right now, he always does, and he is always by your side helping you, and guiding you to be back on the right track again. He wants you to succeed, and live a fulfilling life; one that you can be proud of. To have that happen though, you need to be fully aware of who you are and what your purpose is.

So how does one find their purpose? Well, it starts with looking to your almighty Lord and having a deep-rooted conversation with him. Don't be afraid. He is always there listening, and he wants to help you along every step of your journey. You see, he loves you more than words can describe, and he sees the good you can bring into the world.

It's time you listen to him, and let him guide you. You can talk to him anytime. Day or night, he is listening, and he will help you find the answers you are searching for. Let go of all the fears and questioning of who you can be, and start to truly and deeply connect with God so you can instead know who you are, and be sure of what your purpose in life is.

Comforting Analogy – Myles Munroe

When GOD wanted to create fish, he spoke to the sea. When GOD wanted to create trees, he spoke to earth. But when GOD wanted to create *man*, he turned to HIMSELF.

So GOD said: "Let us (God the Father, God the Son, God the Holy spirit) make man in our image, after our likeness."

Note:
- If you take a fish out of the water, it will die; and when you remove a tree from the ground, it also dies.
- Likewise, when man disconnects himself from GOD, he dies. Spiritually before physical death.
- GOD is our natural environment. We were created to *live in HIS presence.
- We must be connected to HIM because only with HIM does life exist.
- Let us remain connected with GOD.
- Let us remember that water without fish is still water, but fish without water is nothing.
- The soil without the tree is still soil, but the tree without the soil is nothing....
- God without man is still God, but man without GOD is nothing.

Benefits of knowing your identity or who you are:

- Identity helps you understand and appreciate your self worth.
- Identity helps you celebrate your uniqueness, differences, and accept others for who they are.
- Identity is your true joy regardless of your problems.
- Identity helps you appreciate God, and those around you.
- Identity prepares you to live on purpose and fulfillment.
- Identity helps you help others without jealousy, and manipulation.
- Identity helps you to be focus.
- Identity helps you overcome unnecessary stresses in life.
- Identity helps you to maintain peace within and with others.
- Identity helps you to become who you are created to be.
- Identity creates joy, and peace that can't be explained by words.
- Identity helps you to be confident.
- Identity is your true freedom in life and God.
- Identity helps you end confusion, and competition.
- Identity helps you fulfill your true purpose, and calling.
- Identity sets you apart from the crowd.
- Identity helps you find true life reality.
- Identity helps you not to give up.
- Identity helps to strengthen you and your foundation.
- Identity helps you overcome challenges, and competition.
- Identity helps you find your place in God and life.

(John 4:24) – "God is spirit, and those who worship him must worship in spirit and truth."

Notes

Notes

Chapter Five
The Church

"Don't fear, because I am with you; don't be afraid,
for I am your God. I will strengthen you, I will surely help you;
I will hold you with my righteous strong hand."
— Isaiah 41:10

5

Within the church, there is one body, and one spirit just as there is also one hope that belongs to the calling you received. There's one Lord, one faith, one baptism, one God, and the Father of us all who is above all, powerful over all, living in us all, and his favor is given to us all individually and collectively according to God's riches in glory through our Lord Jesus Christ.

The church is not a building but, instead, we are the church.

(1 Cor 6:19-20) - Our body is where God's spirit lives in us, and it's stated in **John 4:24,** God is spirit and those who worship him must worship him in spirit and truth. When we accept Jesus Christ, and accept him as our Lord and Savior, it is the beginning stage that brings us in union with God.

It is a place for growth and training in the ways of God; to overcome our fleshly nature ... to mature into kingdom citizens, and to do kingdom business with clarity all while knowing why we're here and fulfilling our cause of existence or purpose.

No matter how alone you may feel in the vast space that surrounds you, you are surrounded by love, and that love is the purest of all. If you ever need to talk to the Lord, the church is your home to communicate with him. He is always there to answer your prayers, and your questions. As you will read through this chapter, you will understand that God will give you the strength you need to carry through and keep living your path ... your destiny. He is your savior, and through his words and beliefs, you can not only change and better yourself, you can help to change others as well.

The church is God's family. For this reason, seeing the greatness of being built together in Christ is most important. Every family in heaven and on Earth is named under God, and through faith rooted in love and in our hearts. The church is the place where you can get your thoughts out and consult with the Father. All questions are answered in the kingdom of the Lord. He is there to help you at any moment, and any event in your life. If you struggle, He is there. If you need to seek advice from him, he is there. Anything you need, you have his voice inside you and he is waiting for you to return in honesty and truth.

(Ephesians 3:14-21) - [14] For this reason I kneel before the Father,

[15] from whom every family in heaven and on earth derives its name.

[16] I pray that out of his glorious riches he may strengthen you with power through his Spirit in your inner being,

[17] so that Christ may dwell in your hearts through faith. And I pray that you, being rooted and established in love,

[18] may have power, together with all the Lord's holy people, to grasp how wide and long and high and deep is the love of Christ,

[19] and to know this love that surpasses knowledge—that you may be filled to the measure of all the fullness of God.

[20] Now to him who is able to do immeasurably more than all we ask or imagine, according to his power that is at work within us,

[21] to him be glory in the church and in Christ Jesus throughout all generations, for ever and ever! Amen.

It is a place of unity living with complete lawlessness of mind, humility meekness, submission, gentleness, mildness, and patience. It is the place of role modeling, and teaching others to lead by example. The church is a place to mentor, a place to monitor, and a place to motivate. It has a special place in everyone's heart as it is the home for all. It is the home of unconditional love, and learning to love all, especially God with all your heart, all your soul, and with all your strength.

Fruits of Unity

(Romans 12:1-2) - Therefore, I urge you, brothers and sisters, in view of God's mercy, to offer your bodies as a living sacrifice, holy and pleasing to God—this is your true and proper worship. [2] Do not conform to the pattern of this world, but be transformed by the renewing of your mind. Then you will be able to test and approve what God's will is—his good, pleasing and perfect will.

When you think of unity, you may picture everything, or everyone the exact same; however, unity is not about being identical. God did not make us to all be exactly the same. We are all meant to have differences; different ideas, different ways of living, and different physical appearances. We are all meant to follow a unique path, but the goal of the unique path is to find the end goal of reaching God and being with him for all eternity.

Life on Earth is just the first stop for you on your lengthy journey. Here on Earth is where you connect with others and help them to understand God's way, and how life-changing it can be.

Instead of disconnecting with people, you should be constantly connecting, and encouraging others to use their gifts and talents to fulfill God's call in their lives and building up the body of Christ for the work of ministry. Keep encouraging them to take their place in God; as it's said in his word, there are different gifts. Everyone has their own path ... their own journey to take. Yours is individually yours, but you can help others along on their own path to righteousness. That is what unity is all about.

(John 10:27-30) - [27] My sheep listen to my voice; I know them, and they follow me. [28] I give them eternal life, and they shall never perish; no one will snatch them out of my hand. [29] My Father, who has given them to me, is greater than all; no one can snatch them out of my Father's hand. [30] I and the Father are one."

Being one of God's children is an experience like no other. If you are lost, there is someone who can help you find your way. If you are scared, there is someone who can give you comfort. If you are hungry, there is someone who will feed you. That is what is so special about the unity we share with God. Every child of God has a connection to the next. We are all meant to help one another, and help to create a beautiful world.

Unity is community. It is about bringing all people together. To work together, love together, and better their lives together. With more people on the same page, anything is possible. When you have everyone following the same path of God, his path stays bright and true.

(Hebrews 4:10-12) - [10] for anyone who enters God's rest also rests from their works, just as God did from his.

[11] Let us, therefore, make every effort to enter that rest, so that no one will perish by following their example of disobedience.

[12] For the word of God is alive and active. Sharper than any double-edged sword, it penetrates even to dividing soul and spirit, joints and marrow; it judges the thoughts and attitudes of the heart.

Fruits of New Self vs. Old Self

Your life is built up of many stages, and this includes your stages in faith. As you grow and become more aware of yourself, as well as God's ways around you, you gradually change and grow. You constantly become a better version of yourself, and despite sometimes losing your way, but the word helps you find a way to shed the skin of your old self to become the newest and truest version of yourself by following Jesus's pattern. and the Holy Spirit guidance, and repentance.

Knowing your true identity is crucial because when you are successful without knowing your true identity or self, it is far too simple to get out of truth because the foundation becomes shaky and unstable. Our identity helps to give us focus and clarity in all we do despite what comes our way.

(Ephesians 4:1-7) - As a prisoner for the Lord, then, I urge you to live a life worthy of the calling you have received.

² Be completely humble and gentle; be patient, bearing with one another in love.

³ Make every effort to keep the unity of the Spirit through the bond of peace.

⁴ There is one body and one Spirit, just as you were called to one hope when you were called;

⁵ one Lord, one faith, one baptism;

⁶ one God and Father of all, who is over all and through all and in all.

⁷ But to each one of us grace has been given as Christ apportioned it.

When you become your newest, truest self, you become the person the Lord created you to be. You become the child our Father has always seen you as. This is when you have the chance to show others the right path to take, and when you can continue to spread his word. When you continue to share the love, anything becomes possible. The world can become a better place, and each and every single person can learn what the warmth of the Lord truly feels like.

Your plan was made clear from the second you were created. God gave you all the ability in the world to create not only an amazing life for yourself, but for others too. So what are you waiting for? Why are you stalling any longer? Your answers are right in front of you, just waiting to be discovered. God is waiting to see his love spread onto others, and you are the connection to make that happen. Can you feel his love? Spread the word! It is your calling!

(Luke 10:27) - He answered, "'Love the Lord your God with all your heart and with all your soul and with all your strength and with all your mind'; and, 'Love your neighbor as yourself.'"

The Stages of Discipleship

Stage One: Choosing to become a follower of Jesus, and seeking out your spirituality – This is the first step in becoming a disciple of God. This is when you decide this is the path you want to take, and you have an interest in not only bettering yourself, but others as well.

Stage Two: Building a solid foundation in your spirituality and love for God, and learning to understand the ways of a believer – This is when you dig deep into your spirituality, and truly understand God's plan for you.

Stage Three: Growing into your spirituality and desiring God and his ways of living/learning – In this stage, you continue to grow into your spirituality, and learn to not only live for God, but also spread his word and start to understand the importance of helping others find their way to the Lord.

Stage Four: The Mature Disciple – This is one who understands fully the ways of the Lord, yet still has a lot to learn as a follower of God in the young adult stage. They know the path to take, and have taken the right steps, but are still in the early stages of their discipleship, and are not yet ready to show others the right path or journey to take.

Stage Five: The Teacher – This is where you become a disciple of God, and are a parent to others so you can teach them the ways of the Lord. This is when you take the next step of changing from student to teacher.

Notes

Chapter Six

The Kingdom

"The only way the kingdom of God is going to be manifest in this world before Christ comes is if we manifest it by the way we live as citizens of heaven and subjects of the King."
— R.C. Sproul

6

"There can be no Kingdom of God in the world without the Kingdom of God in our hearts."
- Albert Schweitzer

N o matter who you are, and where your path has led you, your place in the church is a permanent one for you are always a part of the Lord's kingdom. His kingdom is a place of being able to find peace and rest of Christ with God. The kingdom is a place of fruitfulness. It is your home … your comfort.

The kingdom is a government of God in authority and a place of peace reigning with Christ and in alignment with the Father. It is a place of sonship; a place of living sacrifice, of righteousness, peace, and joy in the Holy Spirit. It is a place of light, gratitude, and learning to give thanks in all situations, whether they are good or bad. It's a place of intentional and purposeful living. A place of fulfillment and balance in the circles of life and boldness to stand with the truth regardless of the situation or the outcome.

"Jesus made clear that the Kingdom of God is organic and not organizational. It grows like a seed and it works like leaven: secretly, invisibly, surprisingly, and irresistibly." - **Os Guinness**

The kingdom of God is full of surprises that you have yet to uncover. It is the place where your dreams can come true, and you can discover the person you were always meant to be. It is the discovery of your truest self, and the truest form of living. You may be wondering ... is the kingdom only for you? The answer to this is no. The kingdom is for every person, young and old. His kingdom is made to fit everyone and to not only appreciate others' differences, but to embrace them so you can not only live for the Lord, but love him as well.

Simply put, God wants us to live a virtuous life, and one that he would be proud to see. He wants us all to find our way, and to live a life in happiness and peace. When you embrace what the Lord has to offer, and open your arms to him wholeheartedly, his love can be felt all around you, and within you. You can feel his love in the trees, in the air you breathe, and in the smiles that pass you.

Have you been feeling lost lately? Perhaps wondering where your path is meant to take you? It is time that you stop waiting for the answers to come to you. God is right there with you, and he is waiting for you to communicate with him. Let him in, and let the kingdom of the Lord in. Life is a thing of beauty; you just need to take the time to see it.

(Romans 14:17) - "For the Kingdom of God is not a matter of what we eat or drink, but of living a life of goodness and peace and joy in the Holy Spirit." No one will ever find peace in this world without putting our faith in God. God's spirit gives us peace that surpasses human understanding in all areas of life.

God's Government - Theocracy

(Genesis 17:6) – "I will make you very fruitful; I will make nations of you, and kings will come from you."

God has always had a plan for us. He created us all perfectly in his image so we could continue to spread his word generation after generation, and thousands of years down the line. Along with creating the beautiful world we stand on, he also gave us a government to follow. This government, also known as theocracy is a type of guideline for all of us to follow, and is a way for us to come together as one to live for our Father, and help others to understand our reason for living.

Within the Bible, there are many ways that God teaches us what his government is, and what laws are meant to be followed. Below, are some of his teachings, as well as what you can really take from it to benefit yourself, and your life:

God teaches and disciples all the rulers of the world.

In His eyes, the main purposes of governing people are to applaud, encourage, and commend all good, disapprove and punish all evil, always strive for peace.

The government can do many things, but it cannot change wrongs that have already been made, and it cannot take sin away from the heart or soul; this is something only God can do.

When you disobey any government, including the human government, you are disobeying the words and wants of God – it is our obligation to honor, respect, and obey the words, and government of the Lord.

While God started out only making one nation to govern, his plan was to make all nations come together as one so we can all follow his word, and so he can love us all equally.

(Daniel 7:27) – "Then the sovereignty, power and greatness of all the kingdoms under heaven will be handed over to the holy people of the most high. His kingdom will be an everlasting kingdom, and all rulers will worship and obey him."

Royal Priesthood

(1 Peter 2:9) - "But you are a chosen race, a royal priesthood, a holy nation, a people for his own possession, that you may proclaim the excellencies of him who called you out of darkness into his marvelous light."

In the verse above, Peter begins explaining God's relationship and connection to Israel. This is where it all began. This is where people became believers, and the church was something sacred. Just like the people of Israel, we are all chosen. We are all people of the Lord; therefore, we are all connected and a part of the royal priesthood. When the verse states that, "**You** are a chosen race," Peter is speaking to all people, and sharing that we are all a part of his holy nation.

Christians one and all are a part of the priesthood. All believers of the Lord are brought into this priesthood with love and open arms. This is what the Lord's love does for us. It is life-changing. It gives us all a path, a way of living, and an opportunity to create a beautiful life for yourself, and others around you.

Empowerment

(Joshua 1:9) – "Have I not commanded you? Be strong and courageous. Do not be frightened, and do not be dismayed, for the LORD your God is with you wherever you go."

It is difficult to feel alone when you know you have God by your side. It is hard to feel unwanted and unloved when you have his hand in yours with every single step you take. As much as you feel at times like you are lost and left to find your own way, he is always there guiding you. You may not see him, but you can always feel him. His warmth is like no other, and it is there to show you the life you are meant to lead.

There is no reason to feel afraid ... this is the time to feel empowered, and feel like you are part of a very special group. One that wants love and peace for all. Keep staying strong and keep believing in him. When you feel like you can go no further, he will pick you up and give you the strength to keep moving. You are his child as you know, and that bond can never be broken.

(John 5:17-19) – "17 In his defense Jesus said to them, "My Father is always at his work to this very day, and I too am working."

18 For this reason they tried all the more to kill him; not only was he breaking the Sabbath, but he was even calling God his own Father, making himself equal with God.

19 Jesus gave them this answer: "Very truly I tell you, the Son can do nothing by himself; he can do only what he sees his Father doing, because whatever the Father does the Son also does."

Isn't it empowering to see that his love spreads through the masses so quickly? His love started with the son of God, and it continued to move through every single person who let him in. You see, you need to accept his love and support for him to stay by your side. Jesus never lost sight of who his father was, and he believed in him even when it brought him pain and suffering for he knew something better and greater was to come. This is the same for you.

We have a journey to take, and it's our choice how much we let God into our lives. Even though you may question his guidance at times, he knows you better than anyone you have come into contact with, or ever will, and the more you bring him into your life, the more you will increasingly become empowered, and ready to take control of your life, and make a better tomorrow not only for you, but for your friends, family, and even people you have yet to meet.

(John 14:12) – "Very truly I tell you, whoever believes in me will do the works I have been doing, and they will do even greater things than these, because I am going to the Father."

"It is not what we do that matters, but what a sovereign God chooses to do through us. God doesn't want our success; He wants us. He doesn't demand our achievements; He demands our obedience. The Kingdom of God is a kingdom of paradox, where through the ugly defeat of a cross, a holy God is utterly glorified. Victory comes through defeat; healing through brokenness; finding self through losing self." - **Charles Colson**

Notes

_____

_____

_____

_____

_____

_____

_____

_____

_____

_____

_____

_____

_____

_____

Notes

_____

_____

_____

_____

_____

_____

_____

_____

_____

_____

_____

_____

_____

Chapter Seven

Purpose

*"There is no greater gift you can give or receive
than to honor your calling. It's why you were born.
And how you become most truly alive."*
– Oprah Winfrey

7

"For I know the plans I have for you, declares the Lᴏʀᴅ, plans for welfare and not for evil, to give you a future and a hope."
(Jeremiah 29:11)

We are all here for a reason. We all have a purpose. Whether you are religious, spiritual, or haven't yet considered it, everyone questions their reason for being on this planet at some point in their life, and for many of us, we turn to our relationship with God for the answers.

You see, we are not here by coincidence. It was not an accident we are all standing on the same ground. Your birth, and your existence was all part of God's great plan, and you, just like all of his children, have a purpose, and that is to live your life to the fullest while spreading his good words and plan to others.

Even before man existed, before animals existed, and before greenery was on this earth, God had a plan. He knew what his ultimate goal was, and he knew what help was needed. God's work does not just end with him … it continues on with each and every one of his children. It passes on to each generation, and with each new birth, he shows us our path, and the good it brings us.

God does not just want us to live. He wants us to be successful, and to live our lives in the purest way possible. He wants a future for all of us, and all he has asked of us is to nurture our relationship with him. To give him constant love and care. To show him that we appreciate all he has done for us. To continue to spread his word by being fruitful in all areas of life, and bringing new generations into this world. He wants us to fill his world with all his children so we can continue to grow and share his words and love.

(Genesis 1:38) – "And God blessed them. And God said to them, "Be fruitful and multiply and fill the earth and subdue it, and have dominion over the fish of the sea and over the birds of the heavens and over every living thing that moves on the earth." Note our dominion is not over people but our giftings.

Just look around you. This ground you stand on is proof of how much God loves us and what we are meant to do with our lives. Not only are we meant to spread his word as that has been made abundantly clear, we are also meant to care for what we have been given, and to love like him, care like him, and be a little more like him each and every day.

It's so easy for our minds to run astray when we are busy living each day away from the Lord. That is why it is so necessary for you to remind yourself each day why you were put on this beautiful earth, and what God has given you. Nothing that man gives you can compare to what the Lord can give you in either life or death. At any point in your life, he is there. Even when you don't think you need him, he is there.

(Colossians 3:23) – "Whatever you do, work heartily, as for the Lord and not for men."

So why are we here?

Ultimately, it is clear that God had a purpose for creating all of this. He did not want all his creations to be left to wither away. Instead, he needs us all to work together to create a better tomorrow and to live in his presence. He made us all to be like him, and what an amazing blessing that is. We are beautifully made and loved by him equally but we can accept his Love or reject it. Let it be known. Let his word spread through the masses so generation after generation can keep knowing his name. purpose, and knowing the gifts he has given us.

"The meaning of life lies in the quest for something eternally unachievable: divine perfection. For only the impossible is real, and what is furthest from us is in fact closest to us. This would seem to be absurd, but it isn't, for things are not as we see them. Those who reach for the unachievable, the perfection of God, remembering that they were created in his image, are the ones who live in reality.

Since they have placed the Creator at the center of their life, he takes part in what they do, in everything they bring into being. He is present in their every thought and feeling. They were thinking it was impossible to meet God, to become one with him, but in fact this meeting, this union, happens every day, without their even realizing it! Every day, they grow in faith, hope and love; every day, light and peace increase within them."

- Omraam Mikhaël Aïvanhov

Service Relationships – Building a Strong Relationship with God

(Jeremiah 1:5) – "Before I formed you in the womb I knew you, and before you were born, I consecrated you; I appointed you a prophet to the nations."

Building a strong relationship or bond with God is one we all want. We all want to be able to hear his voice, and hear him give us the answers we need. He was there before we all existed, and he will be there long after we are gone. He was there when you

71

were created. He gave you life, and gave you a body for your mind and soul. You are his child, and while he loves us all, there may be times where you feel distant from him, and you need to find the path to reconnect with him.

A relationship with God is a relationship like no other. There is no bond on earth that can compare. So, while you may not be able to speak with him face to face, there are ways you can connect with him and strengthen the relationship you seek to repair with the Lord.

Here are a few simple ways you can strengthen your relationship with our heavenly Father to have a more loving close connection:

Serve others – God is one that has never stopped serving others. The best way to connect with him is to do the same and follow in his path. When you serve others, and care for someone else, you show not only the Lord, but also yourself that you are someone who truly wants to serve the him and do what is best for him and every one of his children.

Read the scriptures – If you are ever feeling lost, or unsure of what the answer is, the scriptures sometimes hold the key. It is filled with knowledge that can help you at any point in your life, and with any struggle. If you want to know how to be closer to God, this is the best place to find your answers.

Talk to the Lord through daily prayer – While you may not be able to physically hear his voice, prayer is a way you can connect with the Lord, and converse with him. If you need guidance, you can ask him for answers, and you can trust that he will find a way to give you those answers.

Reflection – Life does not slow down. There is not a pause button. There is not a way to just take a short break on living your life. So, when you feel lost, and you really are looking for a way to strengthen your connection with God, look upon yourself to reflect on each day, and reflect on how your life is going. Just take time, slow down, and see the beauty in each day.

(Proverbs 3:5-6) – "Trust in the Lord with all your heart and lean not on your own understanding; in all your ways submit to him, and he will make your paths straight."

Three Major Types of Relationships

Traditional Relationships – Traditional relationships are the typical relationships you picture when you think of a marriage or a new connection. It is one that is based on similar interests and personality types. Usually, people connect with someone they have things in common with, and that is what people in traditional relationships search for.

In these relationships, just like any relationship, struggles or issues can arise, and for some, these struggles are put on the back burner, or ignored to try and move past said struggle. This is a routine that most get used to, and with time, this traditional type of relationship becomes a safe and secure spot for an individual. While you can move up to the next two levels of relationships, many stay in this spot because it's comfort to them. It's familiarity.

Conscious Relationships – The conscious relationship is one that takes it to that next level. It gets you to take a look at the spiritual and emotional side of each person to help you understand what you both truly want and need. This is when you realize you have found your soulmate. The one person who truly understands you, and connects with you on a deeper level than you have ever experienced. This is when the relationship changes from an "I" based relationship to a "we" based relationship. This is when you need to not only care for yourself and your own needs, but your partner's as well.

Transcendent Relationships – This is when you fully understand who your partner is and you accept them for all their flaws and strengths. You see who they are, and you love every part of them. The transcendent relationship is the strongest of all, and it connects your souls together as one. You are not only their partner in life, you are their partner on every level. You love them in life, and you love them in death. At this stage in the relationship, there is unconditional acceptance and you can feel free to express yourself as you truly are.

The Three Types of Love

Eros: This is the idea of "physical" love – love that can be seen, or touched. It is based off of feelings, and focuses more on yourself and the selfish side of love. While this is not necessarily a negative type of love, it is more focused on yourself, and can be conditional. There may be reasons why said love exists whether it is based on pure attraction, or the love benefits you in some way. The main idea of this type of love is that you get something from it, and it makes you feel good in general.

Philia (Philos): This type of love integrates your caring side for other people. Instead of it being more focused on yourself, this type of love has you focus on not just yourself, but others around you as well. This type of love is all about caring for one another, and accepting people for who they are.

This love is unconditional and does not require you to get something out of it, because it is a type of love that is based on either common interests, similar personalities, or just a genuine interest in or care for the other person. While this love is not considered selfish, it does require some give and take, which means that both parties need to put in an equal amount of effort to get the same good out of it.

Agape: This type of love is the purest form of love that exists. This is God's love, and there is no stronger form of love than his. His love trumps all, and it is one that cannot be ignored. You feel it, you see it, and you spread it. His love is meant to be shared, and shown to each person around you. There is no higher form of love than his.

(1 John 4:4-8) – ⁴ You, dear children, are from God and have overcome them, because the one who is in you is greater than the one who is in the world. ⁵ They are from the world and therefore speak from the viewpoint of the world, and the world listens to them. ⁶ We are from God, and whoever knows God listens to us; but whoever is not from God does not listen to us. This is how we recognize the Spirit[a] of truth and the spirit of falsehood.

God's Love and Ours

⁷Dear friends, let us love one another, for love comes from God. Everyone who loves has been born of God and knows God. ⁸ Whoever does not love does not know God, because God is love.

(Proverbs 19:21) – "Many are the plans in a person's heart, but it is the Lord's purpose that prevails."

Notes

_____

_____

_____

_____

_____

_____

_____

_____

_____

_____

_____

_____

_____

Chapter Eight
Potential

"One isn't necessarily born with courage,
but one is born with potential. Without courage,
we cannot practice any other virtue with consistency.
We can't be kind, true, merciful, generous, or honest."
— Maya Angelou

Who We Become

"He was in the world, and the world was made through him, yet the world did not know him. He came to his own, and his own people did not receive him. But to all who did receive him, who believed in his name, he gave the right to become children of God, who were born, not of blood nor of the will of the flesh nor of the will of man, but of God."
(John 1:11-13)

Our lives are filled with endless stages. Even before we exist, God has a plan for us, and that is our first stage in life. Once we are born, we are living our physical life, and passing on only brings us to our spiritual life. We are always his children, whether or not we see it. No matter what stage you are in, you are always a part of him, and who you become in a sense is just another version or stage of your previous self.

When God first created this world, he was not initially accepted by all; nor was Jesus. It took them time to have their voices known and their lessons heard and accepted. God always had a plan for us, but we were not always ready to accept him and bring him into our lives. This is another part of becoming who we are. It took us as human beings time to understand God and know that he is our

Creator, and one that should be listened to and respected. It took us time to become the people who openly want God in our lives.

Who knows where God will take us in years to come. Only he can know. He has the answers for us, and he knows what is best for each and every one of us. Luckily for us, God never leaves our side, and he is always there waiting for us to reach our next stage in life.

(1 Corinthians 6:19-20) – "Do you not know that your bodies are temples of the Holy Spirit, who is in you, whom you have received from God? You are not your own; you were bought a price. Therefore, honor God with your bodies."

When living in your physical body, God wants you to cherish what you have, and care for the body you are in. He made you ... he created you perfectly in his image. Therefore, you should never stray away from him, and always strive to live a life of righteousness. We all falter at times, and that is okay, but it's important to find your way back to God if you ever lose the path you were meant to be on, and show him that you honor and love all he has given you. Your body is the Lord's body ... respect it ... love it ... cherish it.

(1 Corinthians 12:26-27) – "If one member suffers, all suffer together; if one member is honored, all rejoice together. Now you are the body of Christ and individually members of it."

For all of us to reach that next stage in life, we all need to work together, and understand what God wants for us. We cannot do it alone. As it is said in **1 Corinthians 12:26-27**, "If one member suffers, all suffer together; if one member is honored, all rejoice together." It is made clear that if one person is struggling, it can create a chain reaction to have others struggle as well. We are all family, and as with family, we must all work together to create a better tomorrow. We must all live through God and spread his words if we are going to have a future we all want and dream of.

If we all believe in the Lord and what he wants for all of us, we can have a common goal that can push us towards something great. Be united with him, and know that he is there for you no matter how much you may push against him. Be united with all people around you, and share his love with all. Be the voice of the Lord and spread his word to each new generation that comes into this world, and see the good it brings.

(1 Corinthians 6:17) – "But whoever is united with the Lord is one with him in spirit."

Training

(2 Timothy 3:16-17) – "All Scripture is breathed out by God and profitable for teaching, for reproof, for correction, and for training in righteousness, that the man of God may be complete, equipped for every good work."

Training is all around us. Just take a look at how you grew up. For the vast majority of the population, we all entered into some form of schooling around the age of four, and continued that up until around the age of twenty, and many times, past twenty. We are constantly training ourselves to be prepared for life, and to know what to expect for all stages of our lives. Our training helps to get us ready to do God's good work, and better our world for not just tomorrow, but for thousands of years to come.

As mentioned earlier, your physical stage of life is just one you will go through, and within this physical stage of life, your training is meant to prepare you for you entering the spiritual world where you will finally get to be in the Lord's presence and know exactly what is expected of you.

While there is work for you now, you will be rewarded greatly in your next life. You will be rewarded for spreading His word, and helping others find their path. Isn't that the purpose of life? To spread the good word, and to live your life to the fullest while helping others along the way. We are meant to love, live, and be happy all while staying true to what the Lord would want for us. While there may be ups and downs along the path, your path will lead you to a fruitful afterlife; one that you have only dreamed of.

(Hebrews 12:11) – "For the moment all discipline seems painful rather than pleasant, but later it yields the peaceful fruit of righteousness to those who have been trained by it."

So why should you embrace God's training? Why is it beneficial to you? Here are some clear reasons why you should let the Lord's word in and spread it far and wide:

Hard work pays off – Anything that is worth it takes time. If it were easy to reach God, then everyone would live the path of righteousness and stay on that path until leaving the physical world. To reach him, you need to put in the work, and you will see for yourself the good that comes from it.

It comes from a strong place of love – God loves us like no other. His love is the deepest you can ever experience, and unlike anyone else, his love does not fade. His training is an extension of his love and is meant to show us how much he truly cares for us.

His training is not overwhelming or lengthy – While his training does take some work, and it can be difficult at times, it is not lengthy, and you will not find yourself taking an abundance of time to get through each step. Just take a deep breath in, and know that he is by your side helping you.

His training is always meant to be beneficial to you – His training always has a purpose, and a positive one at that. There is always good that comes from his teachings, and all you need to do is open your eyes and your heart to see that his words are both true, and extremely helpful.

He is training us to become His disciples – Have you heard the news? God is training you to be one of his great disciples. There is nothing better than this.

The main purpose is to make all of us an image of Him – Becoming one of his disciples makes you into a perfect image of the Lord. This training helps you to become the person you were always meant to be. This is the end goal. This is warmth. This is love.

(Luke 6:40) – "A disciple is not above his teacher, but everyone when he is fully trained will be like his teacher."

Notes

_____

_____

_____

_____

_____

_____

_____

_____

_____

_____

_____

_____

_____

_____

Chapter Nine

Destiny

"Destiny is not designed by mere mortals like us.
It is crafted by God."
— Rodrigo Duterte

9

Judgments and Judgment Day

**"For we must all appear before the judgment seat of Christ,
so that each of us may receive what is due us for the things
done while in the body, whether good or bad."
(2 Corinthians 5:10)**

One day, a time you have yet to know, you will have to stand before God in the judgment seat, and see if you will enter heaven, God's home. His goal ultimately is for all of us to reach that moment on our path, and the hope is that we will have lived a path of righteousness that would have led us to the Kingdom of Heaven. God wants that for all of his children, but it is only up to you to make it to that stage ... only you can make it to that final stage where you are next to the heavenly father.

This happens for each and every one of his children. We will all come to this point whether we want to or not, so why not live in his image? There is nothing stopping you; only you. Don't you want to feel the warmth from God's love? There is nothing better or greater than the care he has for us.

(1 Corinthians 4:5) – "Therefore judge nothing before the appointed time; wait until the Lord comes. He will bring to light what is hidden in darkness and will expose the motives of the heart. At that time each will receive their praise from God."

While he has the right to judge though, it is best not to judge others for their own choices. Follow the path that is meant for you and avoid trying to change others' paths. That is not part of God's plan for you, nor is it God's plan for them. They will find their way just as you have. Only he can shed light on all the demons and darkness in the world. Only he can decide the fate for each of us. Just focus on you, and keep moving forward.

Not only will your day of judgment come, there will be a time when God will come down and Judgment Day will be placed on every human alive, or up in heaven or down in hell. Every person will be looked at, and he will weigh out all good and bad. That is when he will judge the earth to see if his word has spread through each and every generation to come. Therefore, keep sharing his word, and keep spreading his voice.

Give him what he gave to all of us. Give him love, respect, hope, and care for all. Give him everything he deserves because he has shared very clearly that it will all pay off for us. Eventually, we will all get our reward.

(Psalms 96:13) – "Let all creation rejoice before the LORD, for he comes, he comes to judge the earth. He will judge the world in righteousness and the peoples in his faithfulness."

Our Rewards

(Matthew 16:27) – "For the Son of Man is going to come in his Father's glory with his angels, and then he will reward each person according to what they have done."

As mentioned above, there is a time where we will all be judged, and based on the work we have all done in our lives, we have the chance of getting a reward. Each one of us will be rewarded for implementing God's work into our lives, and all he has ever asked of us was to live our lives in a way that would make him proud. He does not ask for money, or property. He just wants our love. Isn't that beautiful?

So as much as sometimes you want to question God's plan for you, or even question why you should be doing God's work, just remember what the Lord has given you so far. Look around you. Just see how beautiful this earth is. See all he has given all humans. We have intelligence, emotions, and a soul to carry us on even after our physical life. No matter what you do in your life, do it with heart, and do it with God always on your mind.

(Colossians 3:23-24) – "²³ Whatever you do, work at it with all your heart, as working for the Lord, not for human masters, ²⁴ since you know that you will receive an inheritance from the Lord as a reward. It is the Lord Christ you are serving."

Know that all your hard work does not go nowhere. Your work is for the strongest, most powerful reason of all, and our God will explain that all to you when it is your time. For now, be good, be caring, be righteous, and follow the path of the Lord. One day you will see where it leads, and you will be blessed beyond your imagination. Only God knows the plan, and it is one of pure perfection. Just wait and see.

(1 Corinthians 15:58) – "Therefore, my beloved brothers, be steadfast, immovable, always abounding in the work of the Lord, knowing that in the Lord your labor is not in vain."

(2 John 1:8) – "Watch yourselves, so that you may not lose what we have worked for, but may win a full reward."

Bringing in Positivity and Releasing Negativity

(1 Peter 1:8) – "Though you have not seen him, you love him; and even though you do not see him now, you believe in him and are filled with an inexpressible and glorious joy."

Have you taken the time to see the good that comes from bringing positivity into your life? It is fairly simple to see the difference. When you are surrounded by negative energy, it spreads. Your body starts to ache, your mind starts to wander, and you cannot seem to get yourself out of the feeling that something just doesn't seem right. This is what negativity does. It sucks the good feelings out of you, and replaces them with mistrust, anger, and pain. Wouldn't you much rather bring positivity into your life? I think anyone would agree!

God does not see the world in a negative light … it's just not a possibility for him because he only chooses to see good. In His eyes, positivity can surround all of us as long as we let the good in, and accept all he has to offer us. The Spirit is all good emotions, and is there to remind us of the path we should all follow. Without him, we would fade into darkness and there would be no light to shine on our paths. We would be lost without him, so take in all the good, and let go of all the bad that has been holding you back.

(Galatians 5:22) – "But the fruit of the Spirit is love, joy, peace, forbearance, kindness, goodness, faithfulness,"

(Philippians 4:8) – "Finally, brothers and sisters, whatever is true, whatever is noble, whatever is right, whatever is pure, whatever is lovely, whatever is admirable—if anything is excellent or praiseworthy—think about such things."

As said in **Philippians 4:8**, "Whatever is true, whatever is noble, whatever is right, whatever is pure, what is lovely, whatever is admirable – if anything is excellent or praiseworthy, think about such things." The Lord wants us to follow whatever path that he made for us. He does not want us to stray, and he wants us to stay loyal to him for it will all be greatly worth it one day. We will all have a chance to show him all we have done for him, and the more positivity we can bring into our lives, and share with him, the better our reward will be.

If you are happy, and positive, your heart is cheerful. If you heart is cheerful, you have the best medicine you could ever ask for. If you heart is cheerful, your spirit and your soul are full.

If there is some negativity holding you back, it is time you release it and let yourself know you are better than the bad that has been holding you back. You have the opportunity to get back on the path that is meant for you and to stay on the path so you can be in his arms once again. Just remember, bring in the good and stay focused on what your purpose is. God will thank you in ways you can only imagine.

(Proverbs 17:22) – "A cheerful heart is good medicine, but a crushed spirit dries up the bones."

For bonuses go to ...

Eternal Life
By Caleb Davis Bradlee

We shall live again! how true
That all will live once more!
And in a world most grandly new
Will worship and adore.

Life again! yes, with God, the King,
Who takes us from this earth
That he may greater blessings bring
At our eternal birth.

Live again! yes, with Christ, so dear,
Who taught the splendid truth,
And made the fact so very clear,
Of an immortal youth.

Live again! yes, with dear ones gone
So far from mortal sight!
Live where all hearts shall be like one,
Where all is blessed light.

Thanks, God, for this holy peace,
This greatest gift of thine,
That whilst our earthly part must cease,
As angels we shall shine.

Notes

Notes

_____

_____

_____

_____

_____

_____

_____

_____

_____

_____

_____

_____

_____

Chapter Ten
Legacy

"Always do your best in whatever you do.
Set goals and seek challenges. Become a role model for those
coming behind you. And always have God in your heart."
– Charles F. Bolden

10

What We Can Be Remembered for In Life

**"One generation shall commend your works to another,
and shall declare your mighty acts."
(Psalm 145:4)**

All of us want to be remembered for something. We all want to leave behind some kind of legacy, and I would say it's quite consistent the type of legacy we all want to leave behind. I am sure you personally want to have future generations know who you are, and what you did throughout your lifetime. You want to be remembered for making a difference, as well as creating positivity and opportunities for each new generation that is brought onto Earth.

The purpose for each previous generation is to keep sharing their knowledge with the newest generation to come. We are all meant to pass down our skills, beliefs, and advice, and God's words of course are most important. He is the one who knows all, and he can predict what can happen years down the road before it occurs. This is why it is so important to spread his word, and spread the outcome of following the same path as the Lord.

Each new generation deserves the right and opportunity to follow the footsteps that you too have taken at one point in your life, and they should have the choice to listen to God's words, and follow the path that he has chosen for you. This is how righteousness and good passes on, and we all have the opportunity to better our planet and our people.

(Proverbs 20:7) – "The righteous who walks in his integrity—blessed are his children after him!"

You see, the people who follow in his path, and spread his good word to each new generation, they will be rewarded greatly. When it is their time for judgment, the Lord will see all the good they have spread, and the difference they have made in the world. Trust in him. The more you can bring yourself into the light, the better you will feel each and every day.

When it comes to your time to meet him, you will be prepared, and you will have all the answers he requires. Live your life with truth and always look to him for answers. He will guide you, and help you to teach others so they can move on and do the same for the generations after them.

So, what you can be remembered for after your breath is the impact or things you have done to people's lives, and community is what you are remembered for, not your bank account and how much money you have saved but lives you touched while are still alive.

(Philippians 4:9) – "What you have learned and received and heard and seen in me—practice these things, and the God of peace will be with you."

Stages in Faith Development

Within the Christian faith, there are several stages of development to help you understand who you are. These stages, or stepping stones, are steps you can take to further your connection with God, and to help you realize the path that is meant for you. Below are the seven stages of faith development, and what they can do for you:

Stage One: Primal Faith – This is the very start of developing faith. This is usually in children aged 0-3, and while they may have no understanding on faith, or even God yet, they are discovering the reality that surrounds them, and figuring out the stepping stones into starting a life in the light of the Lord.

Stage Two: Imaginative Faith – This stage is when imagination comes into play. Children are usually around the ages of 4-8 within this phase, and they absorb everything, and their faith is more based on how they feel versus necessarily what they know. They are just starting to take in the knowledge that God has shared with us, and while they still have a lot to learn, they are well on their way to understand faith and religion.

Stage Three: Literal Faith – The age range for this stage is around 6-12, and as you may know, this is when children really start to discover a sense of themselves, and who they want to be moving forward. It is when they begin questioning their surroundings or what they hear, and they start to sort out what is best for them, and the path they want to follow.

Stage Four: Conventional Faith – In this stage, children are reaching adulthood, and while they still may only be in the range of 13-20, they are very aware of who they are, and their understanding of faith. They have moved past their parents or family's ideas of faith or religion, and have come up with their own thoughts and beliefs. While it may be similar to their parents, the adolescents in this phase have taken the time to figure it out on their own and know their place in the eyes of God.

Stage Five: Personal Faith – Once reaching adulthood (aged 20 or older), you may come to a point where you question what you have believed up to this point. This is when you may have more of a personal relationship with God instead of a public one where you share your faith with others around you.

Stage Six: Conjunctive or Mystical Faith – This stage usually happens in your thirties when you have taken the time to question all you have gone through and what you truly believe. It is when you start to understand what you want in life, and what the Lord's plan for you is too. This is when you finally start to feel at peace with yourself.

Stage Seven: Universal Faith – This stage is one that does not happen for everyone. This type of faith is one that gives you awareness to God's plan for you, and everyone's. If you do enter into this stage, you will be awoken to the truth about faith and God's presence. This is pure love.

Role Model

(Matthew 5:16) – "In the same way, let your light shine before others, so that they may see your good works and give glory to your Father who is in heaven."

Being remembered in life is not just about spreading the Lord's word, and letting future generations know all he has done for us. It is also about being a good role model, and knowing what it means to be a good influence. You need to teach others what it means to be good, and not only care for yourself, but others as well. You need to be able to let your own light shine, and let new generations see the beauty of it. It's up to you to guide them, and lead them on their way.

With your own children, teach them how to walk on God's path at a young age, so that while they grow up, they understand each and every day that he is guiding them, loving them, and helping them. Teach them to be happy, and respectful. Teach them the instructions that God has left for us. It all starts with you. Be the change that creates new generations of disciples.

(Ephesians 6:4) – "Fathers, do not provoke your children to anger, but bring them up in the discipline and instruction of the Lord."

Remember that at the end of the day, money is not anything. Riches that anyone carries are not anything. What matters is the good you spread. What makes a difference is the light that you share with others. A good name means more than any gold or jewels. A path of righteousness means so much more than a life in sin that makes you a millionaire. Money is only temporary, but God's love is permanent. His love never fades.

(Proverbs 22:1) – "A good name is to be chosen rather than great riches, and favor is better than silver or gold."

Blessed be the people who choose to follow his path, and spread his word to each new person that is born onto this great and beautiful earth. It is far too easy to sit and wait for things to come to you, but the strength that comes from taking control of your life, knowing what God wants for you, and actually taking the stand to spread his word is life-changing and so worth it. You have the choice to create a life of fruitfulness or a life in darkness.

Which one will you choose? Where will your path take you? Only you can decide. While both paths may lead you to some form of success, only one brings you to the light of the Lord. That warmth is unlike anything you can ever experience. Be the one who prospers instead of the one who fades away into the darkness.

(Psalm 1:1-3) – "Blessed is the man who walks not in the counsel of the wicked, nor stands in the way of sinners, nor sits in the seat of scoffers; but his delight is in the law of the LORD, and on his law, he meditates day and night. He is like a tree planted by streams of water that yields its fruit in its season, and its leaf does not wither. In all that he does, he prospers."

Notes

Notes

_____

_____

_____

_____

_____

_____

_____

_____

_____

_____

_____

_____

_____

_____

Author's Note

Welcome back from the personal journey and adventure in getting to know yourself.

Here are some more questions to ponder:

- Who are you, truly? What is your identity?
- Where are you from? What is your origin?
- Why are you here? What is your purpose?
- What can you do while you're still here? What is your potential?
- Where are you going after here? What is your destiny?
- What are you going to be remembered for after you have passed on? What is your legacy?

My personal desire is for you and me to examine ourselves and see what we want to do while we still have the opportunity here, and use our gifts, talents, and time wisely and prayerfully for God's glory, before it's too late. Because the Bible tells us clearly, that day and time is coming like a thief that none of us know except God. If today is our last day on Earth where do you see yourself? I ask myself the same question.

I am prayerfully calling each one of us individually and collectively to find peace with our Father, ourselves, and those around us by God's grace, and mercy which never fails us in any situation if we allow God to have his way and do what he planned for us before creation. Then when that last day comes let's have no regrets in the presence of God but rather have confidence and boldness to give an account of our ways before him as it's written in his word.

Conclusively, I want to invite those who are tired of chasing the wind of life and carrying their own load to come home to our Father who is the only giver of life, peace, and all things, to learn from our master Jesus and the architect of our lives.

Holistically Matthew 6:33, and Matthew 11:28-30.

Let God's love, grace, wisdom, knowledge, understanding, might, power, council, and more rest in us, and through us to manifest God's glory in his creation in Jesus's name. Isaiah 11:2

Salvation: it's not a thought process but confession by our mouth, and believing by faith in our Lord's death, burial, and resurrection which brings us in unity with our Father through his son and our brother Jesus Christ that we may all have our own inheritance in our Father's kingdom. Romans 10:8-10

If you accept Jesus, believe and confess with your own mouth that he died, was buried, and resurrected for you and to set you free from sin by faith, then you are a born again child of God into his kingdom. Now congratulations, and welcome to eternal life in Jesus' name.

Made in the USA
Columbia, SC
09 August 2024

39759177R00070